IBIS

A True Whale Story

by John Himmelman

SCHOLASTIC
HARDCOVER

SCHOLASTIC INC. ● New York

To the people of the Provincetown Center for Coastal Studies,
and, of course,
to Ibis

Library of Congress Cataloging-in-Publication Data

Himmelman, John.
  Ibis A True Whale Story

  Summary: Relates the adventures of a humpback whale
calf that gets tangled in a fishing net and is later
freed by a team of helpful whale watchers.
  1. Humpback whale—Juvenile fiction. [1. Humpback
whale—Fiction. 2. Whales—Fiction] I. Title.
PZ10.3.H565Ib 1990   [E]   89-24394
ISBN 0-590-42848-9

12 11 10 9 8 7 6 5 4   1 2 3 4 5/9

Printed in the U.S.A.

First Scholastic printing, September 1990   36

Designed by Tracy Arnold

Deep in a bay,
off the coast of an old fishing village,
lived a pod of humpback whales.

One of the whales
was a little calf named Ibis.
Ibis was curious about everything in the ocean.

One day she and her friend Blizzard
went out swimming. They saw many kinds of fish.
The most interesting were the starfish.
Ibis liked to look at them.
There was something about their shape
that made her feel good.

As Ibis and Blizzard were drifting over a reef
they heard a strange humming noise.
The two calves looked up to see something
large and dark pass overhead.
It was as big as a whale,
but it wasn't a whale.

The calves were frightened.
They had never seen a boat before.
They swam back to their mothers.

The next day, Ibis went back to the reef.
It wasn't long before another boat came along.
Again, Ibis was scared. But she was curious, too.
She forced herself to swim to the surface.

In the cool, hazy air, she saw several faces
watching her. They didn't look scary.
In fact, they looked very friendly.
Ibis liked them.

In the months that followed, Ibis and her friends
lost their fear of boats. Boats came in many sizes
and shapes, and the people in them always seemed
to enjoy seeing the little whales.

As Ibis grew up, she learned more about the sea.
She knew what kinds of sharks to avoid,
what food was the tastiest,
and, best of all, where to find the most dazzling starfish.
Ibis never got tired of looking at starfish.

People and their boats became a part of her life.
Whenever a boat passed overhead, she swam to the top
to say hello.

One evening, Ibis and Blizzard saw a school of fish
swimming around the bottom of a ship.
Maybe there was something good up there to eat.
They went to find out.

Suddenly Ibis was caught in a fishing net!
She fought to get free. But the more she struggled,
the more tangled up she became.

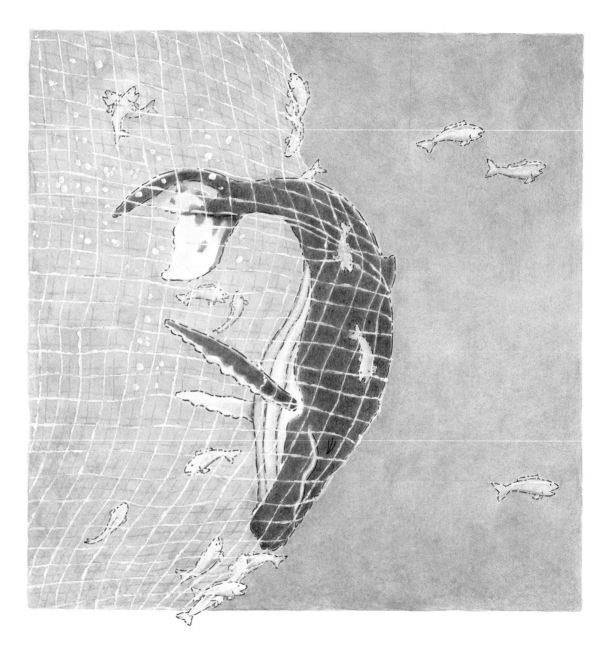

Finally she broke loose, but part of the net
was caught in her mouth and wrapped around her tail.

Blizzard swam off to find help.

Ibis was confused and hurt.
She wanted to get away, far from people
and their boats and nets.
Slowly and painfully she made her way
toward the deep ocean.

Many weeks passed, and Ibis grew very ill.
The net in her mouth made it hard for her to eat.
And every time she went to the surface for air,
the net cut into her tail. But if she didn't
get air every half hour, she would die.

Winter was coming, and it was time for the whales
to move to warmer waters.
But Ibis felt too weak to make the long journey.

Instead she turned back toward the coast.
It was so hard for her to swim,
she could barely keep moving.
Ibis was about to give up.
Then she saw a familiar shape.
It was Blizzard!

Blizzard saw that Ibis needed help.
Gently Blizzard pushed her to the surface
so she could breathe.

Suddenly the water was filled with the sounds
of boat engines.
The whales saw two small rafts
and a boat circling them.

Blizzard and Ibis tried to get away fast.
But Ibis wasn't quick enough.
The boats rushed toward her before she could dive.

The people in the boats began to attach large floats
to the pieces of net that were hurting Ibis.
Blizzard stayed nearby,
circling the boats nervously.

Because of the floats, Ibis could not dive.
She began to panic,
but she did not have the strength to fight.
When the boats came in closer,
a person reached into the water.

Ibis stared at the person's hand.
The hand reminded her of something—
something she loved very much.
She began to feel better.

Soon many hands dipped into the water.
Ibis felt them tugging at the lines of the net.
Moments later the lines fell away, and she was free!

Ibis blew a big spout from her blowhole
as if to say, "Thank you! Thank you!"
Then she dived deep into the water.
For the first time in many weeks, she felt no pain.
She felt wonderful!

Blizzard joined her.
Then the two whales popped back to the surface
for one more look.

The people were waving their starfish-shaped hands.
Ibis knew the hands had helped her,
and that the people were still her friends.

Soon Blizzard and Ibis were leaping and diving
with the other whales, far away in the warm waters
where they would spend the winter together.

AFTERWORD

Ibis (pronounced *eye-biss*) is a real humpback whale. I first saw her one October morning in 1985 when my family and I were aboard a whale-watching ship off the coast of Provincetown, Massachusetts. The whale swam right up to the boat, as if to welcome us to her part of the world. And we soon learned Ibis's story from a marine scientist on board.

He told us that only one year before, Ibis had been caught in the strands of a fisherman's gill net. The scientists who studied the whales in the area found her fighting to surface for air. Several hours later, when she didn't come up, she was believed to have drowned. But shortly afterward, on Thanksgiving Day, a research boat from the Provincetown Center set out to record whale songs. A member of the crew spotted two whales swimming together. One of the whales was trapped in the net. It was Ibis.

The crew rescued her by attaching floats to her net. In this way, they could keep her at the surface so they could reach into the water to free her. She was the first whale ever saved from entanglement! Most are not so lucky. Countless whales have died over the years after accidentally getting caught in gill nets.

As I watched Ibis playing in the water around us, I could understand why those who knew her had fought so hard to save her. And I got the idea to write and illustrate my own version of her story for this book.

Because of the successful rescue of Ibis, the Provincetown Center for Coastal Studies has added an entanglement fund to their program. A portion of my profits from this book will go toward that fund.

Thank you Stormy Mayo, David Mattila, Carol Danton, Mark Gilmore, Mary Pratt, Sharon Pittman, and Charles Mayo, Jr., for the precious life you saved.

And thank you, Ibis, for bringing me a little closer to your world.

John Himmelman